Rachel Isadora
City Seen from A to Z

Greenwillow Books, New York

Library of Congress Cataloging in Publication Data

Isadora, Rachel.
City seen from A to Z
Summary: Twenty-six black-and-white drawings
of scenes of city life suggest words beginning
with each letter of the alphabet.
[1. City and town life—Pictorial works.
2. Alphabet] I. Title.
PZ7.I763Ci 1983 [E] 82-11966
ISBN 0-688-01802-5
ISBN 0-688-01803-3 (lib. bdg.)

For James,
with more than love

Beach ball

Car wash

Dolls

Entrance

Friends

Gallery

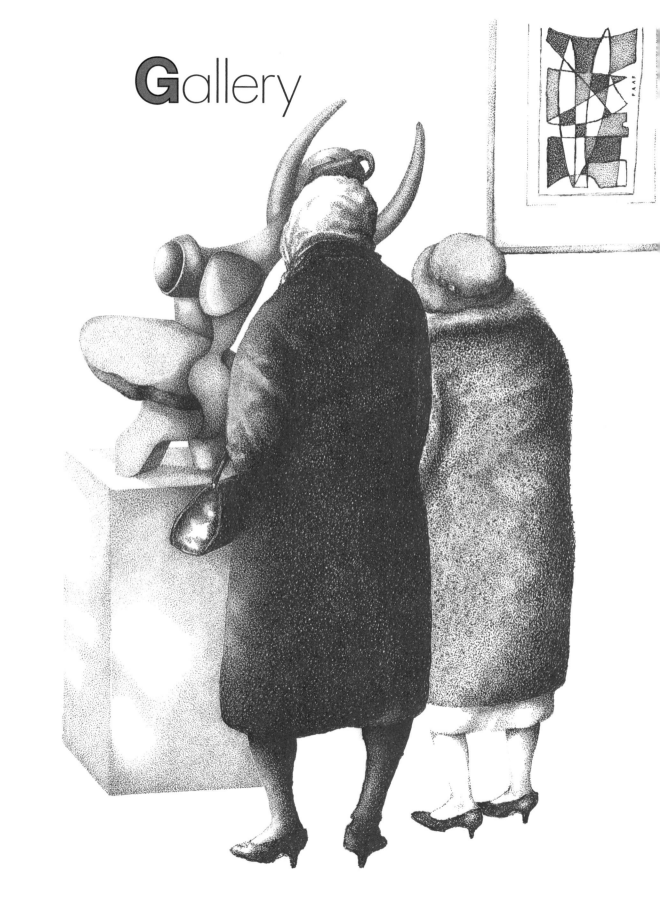

Hat

Ice cream

Jazz

Kitten

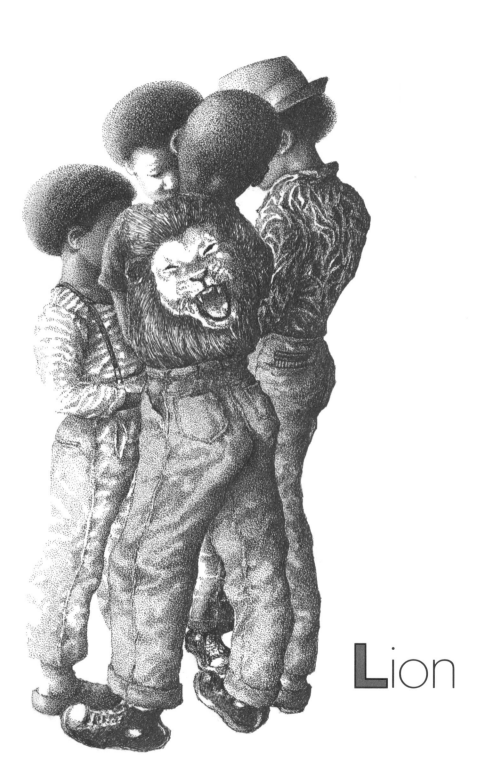

Lion

Music

Ocean

Pigeon

Quiet

Roller skates

Snowman

Tutu

Umbrella

Valentine

Window box

Xmas

Yoyo

Zoo

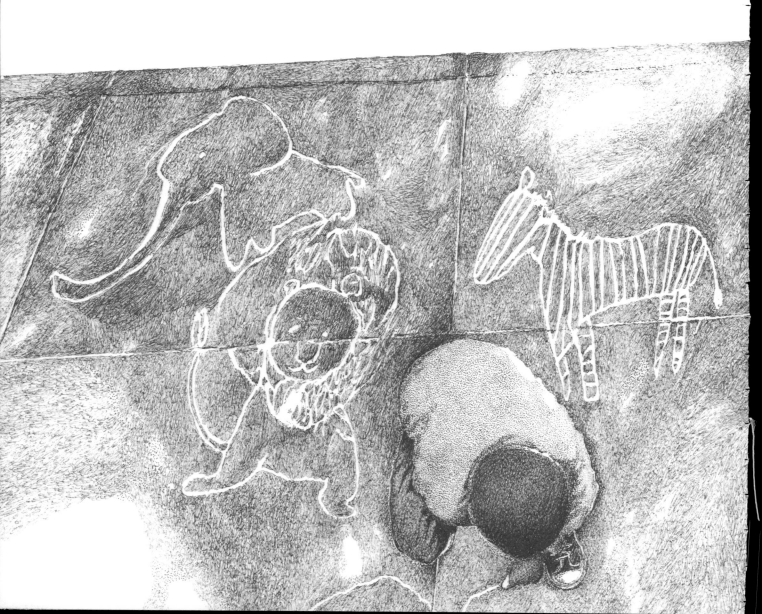